STOP PRESSING

→ YOUR OWN ←

PANIC

BUTTON

A Scientist's Guide to Curing
Anxiety, Ending Panic Attacks, and
Getting Your Dreams Back on Track

RAMSES RODRIGUEZ

Difference Press

McLean, VA, USA

Published 2019

DISCLAIMER

Cover Design: Jennifer Stimson

Editing: Angela Lauria

Author's photo courtesy of: Trung Khong

For my father, Victor M. Rodriguez Lebron,
who always held space for all my panics.

FOREWORD

Biologically, anxiety made perfect sense for our ancestors. Without the conveniences of modern society, we needed to be on alert paying close attention to the environment so we could react quickly. The early humans who survived were the ones who had a lot of anxiety, so it makes sense this trait was passed on to us.

Typically these days, if we are having anxious or even panicky feelings it rarely means there is actual life or death danger. Our own panic buttons are easy to press because we have evolved for them *to* be easy to press. For our ancestors, feeling anxiety meant danger was a foot and triggered physical reactions and hormones to make it easy to fight, flee, or freeze. Exactly how we react to anxiety today and what leads to panic attacks and stolen dreams.

The truth is, anxiety today rarely means there is actual danger. Our brains feel like our life is in jeopardy dozens of times a day but instead of an actual threat, we are worrying about other people's opinions of us, our opinion of ourselves, or, as this book so fascinatingly points out, taking on the stress and anxiety of others around us. We are evolving into another way of using anxiety, but we don't have the training or understanding to know what those feelings of panic mean for our modern evolution. That's why this book is so important and why I wanted every one of the authors we help to understand the role anxiety and panic, about writing a book, or really about almost anything, is actually playing.

Once you recognize that you're feeling anxious there are two options:

Resist or fight it

Accept it

Most people choose option 1. And for years, this was the choice Ramses made that lead to a panic disorder so distressful, prescription medicine seemed like the only option. He resisted his panic attacks, hated them, fought them, acted out, tried to avoid them – anything but accept the anxiety or actively choose to feel or understand it.

This was exactly how I dealt with being over 100 pounds overweight for most of my life. I *hated* being overweight, I hated myself for overeating. I tried to ignore it. I tried to change it. I tried to fix it. Then what happened was I started just overeating all the time and then I could say oh the reason why I'm feeling this is because I'm overweight. I made my weight the reason I was unhappy and then to feel better about being so unhappy I would overeat, gain weight and then get even more unhappy.

Eventually, I caught onto this cycle and vowed to get myself out of the game. This is what happened with Ramses and his panic attacks. Like Ramses, I found I had to use a scientific approach to stop fighting and resisting my problem and instead lean into the problem, accept it, and alchemize it. I was able to permanently change my relationship with my body by accepting my body the way it was in the moment. That was scary because my fear was, if I accept this body I won't change it. If you have trouble with anxiety or panic attacks, it's scary to imagine just accepting them – does that mean they won't change?

As Ramses perfectly details in this book, the exact opposite is true, when you accept something and own something that's when you have all the power to change it.

As a book coach and a publisher, I see anxiety – and more importantly the resistance to anxiety – stopping authors from making the difference they were born to make. I can see how their unique and powerful make up, which leads them to be sensitive to anxiety, is *exactly* what makes them the perfect messenger for their books. In order to be that messenger, they must embrace their anxiety and understand how those sensitives are exactly what their readers need.

Because of Ramses' experience as a working scientist, he was able to objectively observe multiple aspects of anxiety and panic attacks and puts the scientific method to work in order to transmute the negative aspects while strengthening the positive ones. *Stop Pressing Your Own Panic Button* is the book I would want all authors to read when their own "Am I Good Enough?" demons are creating writer's block and stopping them from making the difference they were born to make with a book.

If you are holding this book in your hands now, you are lucky, inside is the recipe to release your anxiety and bring your dreams to life. It might not look exactly how you imagined, but the journey and the results will be well worth it.

Dr. Angela E. Lauria
The Author Incubator
Washington DC
January 1, 2019

TABLE OF CONTENTS

CHAPTER 1

ARE PANIC ATTACKS KILLING YOUR DREAMS?

No one really understands the morning routine of a Panicker getting ready for his or her day unless the person has been a Panicker themselves.

Non-Panickers think we get up the same as everyone else. That we just sit up in bed and take our first yawn and have tons of gratitude for our day in the life.

They believe that we get out of bed, rush to the bathroom, take a shower brush our teeth, and eagerly get dressed for the day. They believe our morning involves a calm breakfast, a hot cup of java, and a steady drive to work listening to NPR or classical music on the radio.

If you are a Panicker, I know you are laughing already.

Our mornings are more like this:

"Shit, I'm awake," you say in your head before your eyes are open. Then there's the struggle to wake up – Panickers pretty much go through the five stages of grief before our feet hit the floor. Even while our eyes are still closed, we are thinking up lines to tell our boss why we couldn't make it into work for the third day in a row, or to tell our spouse why that thing we said for sure we would do this week is still not done. In that moment, we even contemplate going to the doctor, ER, or urgent care so that our reason for breaking our promises can be backed by the diagnosis of a medical professional.

The thing is, what do we tell the doctor?

Our thinking might look something like this: "If I tell the doctor that I just had a rough night, then he will probably think I'm lying and trying to get a prescription or something. I could say I've been suffering from insomnia. After all, it's true, but I don't know if that is a worthy cause for another day off. I'm going to be accused of crying wolf again. I guess I'll suck it up and get on with my damn day."

There really is no peace after we commit to the day. Instead, for Panickers, there is this lingering angst that creeps in our chest. We feel it behind our throat and in our jaw. It's a gut-wrenching anxiety that compresses our lungs and causes our eyebrows to furrow. Imagine that cramped feeling of having to cry, but no tears come out. For Panickers, it's like that all the time.

We walk around saying hi to our families or room-mates (and if we're alone, even to ourselves in the mirror), feigning a kind of normalcy. Inside, we feel like the floor is going to give out at any moment.

There are countless articles calling on workplaces and institutions to respect mental health equally to physical health. As more information comes out about what mental health issues cost employers, there is somewhat of an increase in services and benefits provided, but the truth is, these studies have zero impact on the stigma of being a Panicker. Zero.

My Wake-Up Call

When I was working in research and development in the cancer center in Buffalo, NY, I had to call into work because of a real emergency. I woke up and my eye was swollen shut because I had just developed my very first chalazion. A chalazion, often called a sty, is a benign, painless bump or nodule inside the upper or lower eyelid. The cyst-like lump was clogging one of the ducts in my eyelid and causing my eye to swell up like the rolls on the Michelin tire mascot.

Needless to say, I was not going to slay a dragon this fine day.

I sent an email to my boss explaining that I would not be into work.

At my next weekly meeting, with concern in his eyes, my boss warned, "I just want you to minimize the number of days you call off, because we wouldn't want you to be perceived as undependable and unreliable." He said this even after I showed him a picture of the swelling that I had taken with the selfie cam on my smartphone.

I won't argue here. I can completely understand what my boss was suggesting. Certainly, in my rapidly expanding field of medically-related science, there was a need for the cut-throat gunner scientist. The scientific community is constantly growing and functions under the "publish or perish" mentality.

The truth is, my boss did care about my mental health. He cared about my stress levels. But honestly, only as it pertained to my level of productivity. Employers know that the employee's mental health and well-being will eventually affect how well the company does. And whether your dreams are to rise in your job or your own business, this holds true – your mental health determines your capacity.

Still, his admonishment felt insulting.

Let's take a step back and analyze why the Panicker starts to panic at even the idea of calling out for the day because of a tough morning of anxiety.

When I had the incident with my eye, it was a real problem I had to deal with. I felt like I was being perceived as weak and irresponsible when my boss told me to try not to make this a habit. The panic I was feeling around it was partly about my eye, but even more about the fear of being perceived as weak and irresponsible, which is exactly what happened.

I got angry!

Did he not realize that I didn't pick to have my eye close up that morning!?

Did he want me to make that twenty-minute drive with poor visibility?

Did he not care about me, his subordinate, enough to know that it was in my best interest to address my medical issue?

It dawned on me that despite what all of the definite trend articles are reporting, in the workplace, we are experiencing something different. The truth is, I didn't feel safe expressing that I was a mess all morning. I didn't want to be perceived as the super panicky person who could lose his shit at any moment. I wanted to cover that up.

And this is not limited to gender either. Men and women face different challenges in the workplace. Often times men feel like they will be emasculated in some way if they express their weakness in terms of mental distress. Women face the risk of being dismissed as being weak and not cut out for the job in many of the male-dominated careers.

But here is the thing that happens with the silent Panicker. They are also the silent sufferer.

This is all really amplified with the amount of crap we go through to try to "fix" our panic attacks. Because we don't feel safe feeling vulnerable, we try over and over again to seek relief from the panic attack and constant anxious wheel-grinding that plays in the back of our heads.

Take my client Nicoal. Nicoal had tried medication, breathing exercises, counseling, and even distracting herself from her panics and anxiety.

Nicoal was fifty-two years old when I started working with her in my coaching practice. Her biggest dream at that point was to "not live the last third of my life with this anxiety and panic." She wanted to be able to go out with friends and family and not have to worry about pressing her panic button at a friend's gathering—she even wanted to feel safe enough to take the ceramics class she had always wanted to take. What she realized was that the panic kept getting worse. She felt that the only thing she had left to do was to isolate herself. This client specifically did not want to live the rest of her life with anxiety in panic.

As I worked with her, I realized that she never let herself gravitate toward these things in her life. Her constant fear of panic led her to become, instead, the rescuer of those around her.

I share this to make a point. Notice that Nicoal had been trying many of the standard recommended techniques for treating panic. Even her medications did not work. I hear countless times that medications only cover up the symptoms of panic, and the minute the medications wear off, boom, another panic hits. In some cases, individuals on medications that require strictly regimented intake begin to experience intra-dosage withdrawals in addition to their anxiety and panic symptoms.

One of the hardest things about panic attacks is that they show up differently in different people, often tricking the Panicker into following a red herring because the attack presented atypically.

A standard description of a panic attack includes increased heart rate, increased sweating, chest tightening, and muscle tension. But some individuals experience things that come from an even greater pool of panic symptoms. Some experience full-body muscle rigidity, jaw muscle rigidity and clenching (in a condition called bruxism), body shaking and trembling, airway tightening, differences in body temperature (where the body is cold, but the face is hot), and even stroke-like symptoms. An individual with panics who I interviewed described the stroke-like attack as an upward-moving tingling originating from the base of her spine. The tingling radiated outward towards her limbs resulting in generalized weakness, all the while still experiencing an increased heart rate. Another stroke-like attack was described to me as being just like the one-sided weakness common in stroke, including some facial numbness.

It makes sense that medications are pushed. In some cases, medication is the what doctors are directed to prescribe per American Medical Association protocol.

To be honest, there is a reason why most people don't find permanent relief of their panics. Their jobs are on the line which trickles into financial and even interpersonal relationship issues. There is additional pressure from loved ones and colleagues to seek treatment for the symptoms which can cause additional financial and time-management stress. Often the shame of being a Panicker causes attempts to self-diagnose and self-treat, but without the proper instruction and accountability to have those methods work, they are rarely effective.

Panic keeps on attacking until the Panicker outgrows this rat-race of treatment. Basically, the Panicker ends up waiting for the problem to be *worse* than the solution.

The real reason panic and anxiety lingers, is because the reason the panic has shown up in the first place is not actually being addressed. No amount of drugs or even meditation sessions can stop your panic attacks from coming, unless you find the source and change it.

Looking back to the day my boss cautioned me about missing work, how and why I got there is so clear to me. It wasn't just a medical emergency; it was everything about that situation which triggered my panic and the exact conversation I didn't want to have with my boss. As you read this book, you will be able to put those pieces of the puzzle together for yourself. There are ways you are setting yourself up to fail and to panic, and once you see how you are doing this, you will be able to change it *forever*. But for it to work, you have to be willing to say goodbye to your familiar companion, panic. In the next chapter, I'll share exactly how I did just that.

CHAPTER 2

A SCIENTIST IS BORN

I was always curious as a little kid. I pretended to be Sherlock Holmes in the front yard of my house. I took my parent's cleaning gloves and Ziploc baggies and collected crime scene samples from our garden.

Looking back, I can see it was my way to deal with the constant anxiety I experienced as a child. At the time, I had no idea what was causing my unsettling feeling. I have memories as far back as two years old. I've confirmed the memories by asking my parents, but I remember being left in rooms alone and panicking.

Throughout my life, I developed obsessive compulsive disorder (OCD). I wasn't actually diagnosed with OCD until I participated in a physiology study in college. I had social anxiety and a fear of germs.

Eventually, I came out as a gay man when I transferred to a New York college in 2009. For a small period, my anxiety diminished. I was on cloud nine with my "new" identity. But that really only lasted for about a week; then I realized that I had entered into an identity crisis. I developed an eating disorder in response to the pressures of the gay culture that I was now a part of.

After completing my coursework in music, I decided that I wanted to go to medical school. Oddly enough, when I came out as gay, I got brave enough to tackle my fear of germs with diving into science. That worked. And after all, I never really stopped being curious.

I eventually started dating, and that's when the panic attacks kicked in. I began to have feelings of gloom and doom just like the ones from my childhood memories. I would feel like something terrible was happening to the people around me without obvious evidence to support my suspicions. I would also feel very emotional all of the time.

Friends would often say "you're too sensitive" and that I needed to "grow thicker skin." I remember being extremely volatile with my lab professor. At one point, he mentioned that he didn't even like being around the lab when I was in there because he felt like he was always walking on eggshells around me.

After I received my molecular genetics degree, I decided to continue my education in genetics research. I taught biology and biochemistry labs while in grad school, and then had the opportunity to take my dream job in research and development at the top cancer institute in Buffalo, New York.

I was in the career of my dreams, but these pesky panics were getting in the way. The pattern seemed erratic. I couldn't tell where the panic attacks were coming from and why they were being triggered in odd places like supermarkets and while I was on the road.

It wasn't until I started medication for my panic attacks that I realized that something else was going on. The medication actually worked in a way. I was able to calm down enough to realize there was actually something different about me. I was experiencing events differently than the people around me.

I really started to consider all of the possibilities that could explain my stance with respect to my surrounding. How was I actually experiencing my world around me? Could it be that I wasn't going crazy? Could there actually be something to the feeling of gloom and doom? *Could my panic attacks be serving a purpose?*

When I started to ask this one out-of-the-box question, I unlocked a world of possibilities and treatment options for myself. This tiny bit of gentle curiosity about my suffering with panic attacks opened my heart to the solution I will share with you in this book. Yes! The panic attacks *were* serving a purpose. An amazing one! I actually became grateful to my panic attacks. They weren't random at all – they were my north star and had been all along, from way back when I was two.

As I will explain more in future chapters, the drugs doctors prescribed me ultimately caused more panic and stuck-ness than going without them, but that's not to say drugs never have a place. I am a scientist after all! For me, the brief period of medication allowed me to develop a program that could help people like me be the cure of this curse of a condition. In this book, I will share the steps I discovered. It all starts with gentle curiosity... and so I'm going to invite you to try some of that right now. Take a moment and ask yourself: *If your panic and anxiety was serving a purpose, what might that purpose be?*

Don't worry, you don't have to get the answer to that question right now. All I want is for you to start asking it. As you do, you will plant the seed you need to get to the root cause of your own anxiety. Let me explain how it works.

Chapter 3

FROM PANICS
TO CURED!

I understand that your panics can make you feel all over the place. They can make you feel unhinged in the morning as you get ready for work. They can make you feel like vomiting in the passenger seat of your car as you travel into work. And they can make you feel like you want to run and escape from work – so, now what?

What exactly do you do about all the anxiety? How do you stop the panics in mid-track? How do you prevent them from ruining your morning mojo?

How do you move toward the future you desire without having a panic attack?

Heck, how do you go to the supermarket without having a panic attack?

Well, I have to warn you, the solution is quite counterintuitive.

You may think that what you have to do is push back on the panic attacks. That you have to fight the panic attacks like a newly diagnosed cancer patient takes on a tumor. Or maybe you believe that panic attacks are now an inevitable part of your life and that they are here to stay. They are now the ultimate truth of your life and that there are no options available but a heavy dose of IV Ativan hanging from a bag and into your elbow.

But simply put, all of that mental pushback is actually making the panics worse. *Read that again!*

If you still have panic attacks, it's actually your thoughts about the panic attacks that are making them worse!

The fact that you hate the panic attacks so much makes them more frequent and makes them stronger. The fact that you numb them with medications makes the panics between doses that much worse.

Now, hang in there with me. The reason this seems counter-intuitive is that we are trained to push back directly against something that is unwanted. This permeates throughout society constantly. Let's takes a simple case of spilled milk.

As a child, we are taught that milk is something that we drink for nutritious purposes. Milk is purchased in its container, usually a box carton or a plastic jug, and then it's brought home and stored in the refrigerator. Then when it is time to drink it, the milk is poured out of the jug into a separate drinking container. Babies usually take their milk in a bottle and toddlers in a sippy cup. But what happens when we spill some of that milk? We are taught to clean it up! Spilled milk, however, may only be the last step in the spilling of the milk! What if there was a crack in the bottle? What if the sippy cup lid was loose and not screwed down tightly enough? We don't like the mess that spilled milk causes, so we continually wipe the spill.

This is the problem! We are treating panic attacks like spilled milk. We continuously wipe the symptoms of the panic attacks up and don't address the root cause as to why the attack is spilling into our reality in the first place.

This is why I am so grateful for my experience with anxiety drugs. The job of the drugs was to "wipe up" the mess my anxiety attacks were causing. But when I was on the medication, my panic attacks didn't go away! Because I was trained as a scientist, I started to critically think about what was actually happening. Shortly after I took Xanax, I was not anxious or panicky. But as the time lapsed between doses, my anxiety climbed.

That immediately alerted me to the fact that the medication was numbing something. It was covering up something. Or maybe temporarily shutting something off, some mechanism. The meds and superficial therapies were only curbing the panic, but something from outside was pushing my panic button.

Then I came across a concept that changed the way I saw myself and panic attacks forever.

I was getting a massage, and through casual conversation, my therapist mentioned that maybe I was an empath. This was the first time I had ever heard the term. I looked it up, and I started to realize that I might be perceiving my world differently than the people around me!

I Google searched empaths, and a book by Psychiatrist Dr. Judith Orloff called *The Empath's Survival Guide* popped up. I bought it immediately.

As I read this book, I found myself in complete amazement of what I was reading. I was literally being described in the pages of her book. She described empaths as being individuals who were absorbing the energies of their surroundings and quite literally being affected.

This would explain my emotions and my desire to isolate and why I always felt drained. It would explain why I would panic at supermarkets and at work!

As a scientist, I took this idea of being an empath with a grain of salt. "This is a bunch of 'woo woo' crap that I have no space for! This is really grinding my gears," I thought.

But I kept coming back to the theories my massage therapist casually mentioned. I could not find a way to make sense of this energy "woo-woo" stuff in my head. To be honest, I felt like I was just too smart and too grounded in the scientific background I held. How could I, the molecular geneticist and developmental biologist, really believe that I was being influenced by external energies?

Nikola Tesla Saves the Day!

I was committed to making sense of this for myself. I had to keep an open mind about this whole empath thing because up until that point, nothing else explained what was going on with my random panic attacks.

Surprisingly, one day as I was studying the works of some spiritual leaders for possible explanations that could help me assimilate this "empath" thing, I came across a quote by Serbian scientist Nikola Tesla, which read, "If you want to find the secrets of the Universe, think in terms of energy, frequency, and vibration."

That was my first Eureka moment! That was the first item of knowledge that allowed me to bridge the gap in my understanding of what was going on!

In a subtle but clever way, Nikola Tesla takes a reductionist approach to life. Basically, instead of thinking of everything in terms of actual items in the world, he was saying that everything was energy frequency and vibration.

This is the guy that literally discovered remote technologies, and he was describing the framework for which empathy worked!

So, without getting too much into the science aspects of what he was referring to, I was able to adopt what he was suggesting as the vehicle by which I was being affected and caused to panic as a direct response to my surroundings.

See if you can follow: If *everything* is energy, frequency, and vibration, then it means that *everything* is able to transfer energy as well. This leaves *nothing* out of what is considered to be energy and thus leaves *nothing* out as a possible "thing" that can get transferred. In other words, people's "vibes," their moods, their emotions, their projected thoughts, all have the means to be transfers because they are all energy.

This was how I made sense of the previously "woo-woo" idea of me being an empath with the science I know and believe.

I decided to take a reductionist approach myself and began some experiments to determine what empathy meant for me and how I could rationalize it in my world.

After a series of tests, I determined that I was energy-sensitive. That conclusion unlocked a world of possible of treatment options for my panics that I would not have had otherwise if I had not explored the energetics in a situation.

The reason your panic attacks are not gone is likely the same as mine. What's happening is that your internal machinery for warning is being triggered externally. To change this, you too will need to get to experimenting. In the next several chapters, I'm going to show you how to do just that.

If you are a bit skeptical about the world of metaphysics and woo, don't worry. I'll offer up my explanations about how this all makes sense on a scientific level, while taking you through all of the steps I used to get to a point of not worrying at all about a next panic attack!

CHAPTER 4

THE INTERESTING SCIENCE OF PANICS

Before we get into what can actually be causing you to press your own panic button, it is important to understand a few key concepts that can help you to anchor yourself with the external reality.

Notice that I said, "external reality."

Why is this factor important? Well, up until now, most of the treatments you may have tried have to do with treating the symptoms of the panic. You may be taking drugs that help stabilize the mood or release happy neurotransmitters into your brain, whereby the anxiety attack is curbed temporarily while the drugs are in your system.

You may also be trying breathing techniques aimed at only calming you down by virtue of stabilizing your blood pH.

But what if the cure for your panic attacks has less to do with the panic attacks themselves and more to do with the way you perceive your reality?

What do I mean by this?

Well, to get you to a clear picture of what I mean, I'll give you an example of my client Marina. Marina worked in the biomedical science field for over twenty years. She had been having panic attacks for most of her life (she remembers them starting as early as age five!). Gradually, over the last twenty years, she noticed that she managed her attacks by isolating herself more and more. She didn't even want to go to a painting class that she had been dying to take in the weeks before she reached out to me for help.

When Marina told me this story, I was quickly reminded of myself. I knew exactly what was going on. I had realized that she was reacting to her external environment in a way that most doctors would dismiss.

After my own research and Tesla's findings, I knew Marina was reacting to the energy around her.

I remembered that, as my panic attacks got worse and worse, they were also increasingly less predictable and their cause less certain. As a scientist, I had to start to think outside the box. I was only prescribed ten Xanax a month, and I was having to plan my life around my panics.

Marina was a scientist, too, so I shared with her the idea of being an empath, but since I knew that might be too out-there or spiritual-sounding for her to grasp, I decided to refer to it here by its least common name "energy-sensitive."

I explained to Marina that humans are sensitive to energy. Some are more sensitive than others. I explained that I felt she was an "energy-sensitive" like me. Energy-sensitives are individuals who can intensely perceive the energies around them in a way not limited to their five senses of sight, touch, smell, hearing, and taste. In many cases, energy-sensitives perceive sensory information intensely through the five common sensory organs, but they also perceive energies without using those organs as well.

I told Marina there were some key scientific findings that support the phenomenon of humans experiencing external energies.

We looked at scans of brains. The brain contains an empathy center. The region of the brain that contains the "empathy center" is in the right temporal lobe. The region is called "the theory of mind." This region is responsible for an individual's ability to "get in someone else's shoes," so to speak. Individuals who have suffered trauma in this region of the brain have been shown to have a loss of simple empathy for others.

Marina was on board. The science was there, she was with me. I could tell she had a gentle curiosity about whether, how, and if I was right about my theory.

Just like I asked you to plant a seed of curiosity for yourself earlier in the book, I asked Marina to do the same, and I could tell the pain of her anxiety has reach the point where she was open to trying something different.

I sent Marina off with some dense scientific literature that I'm going to spare you. Basically, the studies I shared with her showed a specialized type of neuron called the mirror-neuron. These neurons fire in the same pattern in an observer as in the subject being observed. In other words, if an ape watches another ape eat a banana, both the observer brain and the subject brain fire similarly. This suggests that observation alone can cause a neurological response, which also lends room for how our bodies could have physiological responses to our external reality.

Another collection of papers I shared with her were in the arena of physics. In physics, waves are described as being constructive or destructive – they either enhance in intensity if they sync up (constructive), or they destroy and collapse each other if they are not in sync (destructive).

Marina was nothing if not a good student, but when she came back to me the next week, she said, "I did the reading you assigned, but I'm not sure I understand what this has to do with me."

"Well, Marina," I explained, "when we apply this work about mirror-neurons and constructive and destructive waves to energy-sensitives, it starts to make sense how specific external energies can really sync up with us and amplify within us. This is how we press our own panic buttons. And now that we know this, there are only a few more steps to stopping!"

Marina was excited. She exclaimed, "I'm ready to stop pressing my own panic button right now!"

As much as I wanted to do that, too, I knew there was more work to do. The next step was to identify specifically what type of energy-sensitive Marina was. And that's what you and I will do together for you in the next chapter.

CHAPTER 5

FEELING THE WORLD AROUND YOU

The moment I was able to understand how energy could be transferred among all things was the moment I was able to really free myself up to all treatment options for my panic attacks.

The next important step is to identify the kind of energy-sensitive you are.

There are three main classes of Energy-sensitives that are worth mentioning here. As I said before, psychiatrist Dr. Judith Orloff, author of *The Empath's Survival Guide,* has done fantastic work in explaining empaths – in this chapter, I will use her explanations to show you my take on how that applies to energy-sensitives.

We energy-sensitives experience the world completely differently than the non-sensitives. There is constant information coming in at us. To be honest, it is likely that non-sensitives also get bombarded with such external energies, but unlike energy-sensitives, their filters for these energies seem to be intact.

Energy-sensitives tend to either experience physical energy or emotional energy from others and are open to intuitive energy perception. As you read through these descriptions, see which most resonate with you. If it sounds like I'm talking about you, I am! Not everyone reads these descriptions and feels like it's about them. In fact, most people will think these descriptions are a bit weird. But if you are this type of energy-sensitive it will hit you right in the gut. Make sure you keep track of which ones fit you. People often have multiple types of energy sensitivities.

The Physical Energy-Sensitive

The physical energy-sensitive is the person who feels so many different physical symptoms in their bodies. They're unable to even understand why they hurt. They notice that after a long day of work they feel like their body had been drained or depleted. They may experience unexplained pains in their body or other unexplained symptoms. Some may quite literally feel like they got hit by a truck. This person is quite often labeled as a hypochondriac by doctors, friends, relatives, or even themselves.

Physical Energy-sensitives may start to notice that when they are around others, they begin to feel unexplained pains. This happened to me when I was working at a cancer institute as a scientist. I remember walking by our department secretary and getting an extreme sense of nausea. By that time, I was already in the process of defining reality as an energy-sensitive. I remember thinking, well, I wasn't nauseous a minute ago, so why do I feel like this now?

I got brave and backtracked towards the secretary and asked, "You wouldn't happen to be feeling nauseous, would you?"

"Yes, Ramses, how the heck did you know that?"

I knew she was a bit spiritual, so I took a chance at explaining to her that I was an energy-sensitive. She then confirmed that she in fact suffered from Meniere's Disease, which is a condition characterized by extreme moments of vertigo (dizziness), and that her flare-up caused her extreme nausea.

As I left her desk, I'll admit that I was a bit freaked out by the experience. I was still in shock that I could have experienced *her* nausea in my body. But I was also relieved. This helped me realize that I was not making this stuff up. That I was picking up symptoms from my surroundings.

The Emotional Energy-Sensitive

The second major type of energy-sensitive is the emotional energy-sensitive. This person feels emotions intensely. They could easily be feeling fine and then quickly be flooded with all sorts of emotions. These emotions seem to come out of nowhere, and they range from mild in intensity to severe. This type of energy-sensitive is often labeled as being "too sensitive" emotionally and is often told things like "get a thicker skin." They may even be clinically diagnosed with mood disorders or even with bipolar disorder.

The emotional energy-sensitive often feels conflicted by their emotional experiences. They usually have no idea why they have sudden shifts in emotion. This happens to me quite often in public places. For example, during the holidays at my local supermarket, I tend to feel many emotions relating to guilt, shame, insecurity, sadness, anger, happiness, joy, and even jealousy. I normally get a flood of emotions that are not related to my initial state upon arriving at the market.

One of my clients, Priya, explained that she did not like to go out to public places because "it felt safer just to stay inside." She identified as an extrovert, but she couldn't understand why lately she was emotionally panicking in public places. She usually feels great around people, but she had been getting so emotionally-charged that she started to isolate in her room.

The emotional energy-sensitive tends to isolate from crowds and feels emotionally overwhelmed when they are around certain people and around crowds.

The Intuitive Energy-Sensitive

The intuitive often feels many types of energies. The origin of these energies can sometimes be complicated to understand. Energies can come in the form of thoughts, emotions, sensations, voices, visions, premonitions, and "vibes" or "ju-ju." To really feel comfortable with this, I really had to understand the principles of energy. Remember, as Tesla suggested, think of everything as energy, frequency, and vibration. This helps the intuitive anchor into their experience. Everything, including thoughts and visions and auditory input, are just focused forms of energy that can also be transferred, and this can still vibrationally average with energy-sensitives.

The intuitive energy-sensitive is often labeled as being too "woo-woo" and in some instances is clinically diagnosed with Schizophrenia.

There are many ways of classifying the types of intuitives. Below I provide a list of my take on the types of intuitive energy-sensitives.

Telepathic Intuitives: These individuals attain information across time and space. They are able to perceive information that is not limited to one location. Precognitive intuitives experience "premonitions" before they occur in the form of thoughts, visions, and/or sounds.

Mediumship Intuitives: These individuals are able to perceive energies (visions, sensations, sounds) that are associated with "the other side." They are able to pick up energetic residues of the deceased in places or surrounding people. This allows them to connect with that organized thought form in a communicative sense.

Environmental Intuitives: These individuals have close connections to nature, earth, and planetary systems. They pick up on subtle shifts in gravitational energies, magnetic energies, and even electric energies. A special case of the environmental intuitive is the *electro-sensitive*. Some of these individuals have many "weird" experiences with electronics. They may feel buzzing or have trouble sleeping with electric thermal blankets or electronics in the room.

Animal Intuitives: These individuals can easily "vibe" with animals. Even the most skittish of pets may be drawn to them. They may experience communication with animals telepathically.

Social Intuitives: These intuitives often can perceive not only emotions but intentions of an area. They may feel like something or someone is loaded with "bad vibes." Usually, these experiences are coupled with telepathic intuitions, but sometimes they feel a feeling of "gloom and doom" without any further energetic input. Sometimes they can go into a room and feel like it has bad "ju ju."

Sexual Intuitives: These individuals can pick up on sexual energies in people. They are often able to perceive when individuals are sexually attracted to them. In relationships, they often easily pick up on their partner's energetic bids for sexual connection.

Nutritional Intuitives: These individuals have extreme sensitivity to food energies. They often gravitate towards a plant-based diet. They are able to feel into emotional states of meat-based protein. Nutritional intuitives also experience many gastro-intestinal reactions and often suffer from IBS or have other nutrient sensitivities. They are also highly reactive to sugar, caffeine, and alcohol. A special type of this intuitive is the *chemi-sensitive*, individuals that are extremely reactive to chemicals in their environment (i.e., odors, medications, etc.).

Notice that many types of energies can be picked up by energy-sensitives. This is part of the reason why some of my panic attack clients have mentioned things like "I just had no idea about why I was constantly triggered or at a persistent state of overwhelm."

I will take this opportunity to highlight that in no way do I advocate for the discontinuation of seeking treatment from a medical professional. I also don't discredit the efficacy of pharmaceutical therapies. Science does a great job at describing the mechanism of how each domino in a panic attack cascade interacts with each other. Pharmaceuticals are very good at intercepting a domino before it hits another domino. Drugs and science can have a role to play in curbing anxiety and panic attacks mechanistically. In essence, a clinical diagnosis can describe which domino is hitting which other domino. Clinicians explain the physical, physiological, neurological, and emotional components of a panic attack as they pertain to the mechanism of perception in the body. The medications and scientific explanations are not at all dismissed here.

But I want to ask a different question with you: What pushes the first domino in the panic attack cascade?

My answer? Energies do!

So, if energies push over that first domino, to stop pressing your own panic button, you need to learn to manage how you respond energetically to external stimulus, especially in the areas you are most energy-sensitive.

CHAPTER 6

DIFFUSING A PANIC ATTACK

Understanding how your body is capable of absorbing and entraining with external energies is crucial to effectively curbing a panic attack as it starts. At the beginning, most of my clients have elevated anxiety and anxiety attacks, but as they begin to understand how their external realities are affecting their current state, they are much better able to assuage their panics.

In this chapter, I will offer my A.C.T. Now method for triaging and curbing your panic attack as it is in progress. To apply these methods, however, we must consider first how one type of energy permeates through all panics. This is emotional energy. This emotional energy can be generated internally or externally.

External emotions come from experiencing a huge influx of other people's emotions that makes your nervous system come to a state of overwhelm.

Internal emotions usually arise due to your own thoughts.

In the last chapter, we reviewed the various ways external emotions can trigger anxiety to energy-sensitives. But there is another piece of the equation you need to understand before you can apply the A.C.T. Now method for triaging and curbing panic attacks.

How Internal Emotions Can Trigger Panic

Internal emotions usually arise due to thoughts. Let me give you an example of how your thoughts can cause extreme emotions that lead to anxiety and can climax into a state of panic.

Take the case of money. You may think that you don't have enough money to pay a bill next month. Or you don't know how you will come up with the money to send your child to their favorite summer camp, deadline approaching in a few months. Well, the thoughts that you have are about money, but the emotions that arise are feelings of shame, guilt, and anger.

You feel shame because, as social being, we believe that the parent or head of household is solely responsible for providing funds for all the desired ventures in the home. Guilt comes as a result of thinking about the sad expression on your child's face when you explain that you do not have enough money to send him or her away to soccer camp. Anger then develops as a result of the shame and guilt. Anger is what is often referred as a cover emotion, a term coined by author Teal Swan in her book *The Completion Process*. Anger covers up emotions of insecurity and vulnerability and usually indicates that there are root emotions that can be integrated, a topic that I will reserve for Chapter 12.

Notice what is going on here. All that is happening here is a set of thoughts. All of these thoughts are of how we *believe* we should be behaving. Most importantly, the thoughts have nothing to do with the present moment. The thoughts are of the past and how things should have happened, or of the future, which are thoughts of what might happen.

The truth is, in the moment you are thinking these thoughts, your body is actually safe, but the thoughts are causing the emotions propelling the anxiety which leads to panics. Anxiety is a feeling state that is perpetuated by the inability to remain focused in the present moment and is initiated by the negative emotions felt as a result of thoughts regarding one's past or future events. The anxiety you experience comes to a climax in the form of a panic attack.

The A.C.T. Now Method for Triaging Your Panic Attacks

Whether the anxiety comes from internally or externally generated emotions, it is important to approach yourself during a panic with as much gentleness as possible. We have all heard the phrase "you are your own worst enemy," right? When dealing with a panic attack, this is especially true. Lets face it, we often tell ourselves that we shouldn't be having panics. I remember feeling embarrassed while having one. My thought was that I should not be going through this because I was "stronger than this." Whether the original emotional energy was external or internal, I was creating internal emotional energy that was fueling the fire of my panic attack. I had become my own worst enemy.

The way to curb the panic is actually counter-intuitive to that natural instinct to blame and criticize yourself. This is what makes it so tricky to solve, and why no amount of breathwork or Xanax will ever be enough if you are continuing the self-blame approach.

In order to finally solve your panic attack problem, you must reverse your attacks on yourself from your own mind. As you start to feel the panic come on, *remember* the phrase "A.C.T. Now," which is a three-step process for curbing your panic attack.

A: Acknowledge the Panic

In this step you will acknowledge that you are having a panic attack. This is simple, but often we get so caught up in the physical sensations that we don't acknowledge that our body is being completely consumed by this physiological response that is the panic attack. This immediately helps you place your attention on yourself and helps you direct your energy towards feeling better as smoothly and quickly as possible. This step sounds like this:

"Okay, I am having a panic attack."

C: Compassionately Validate Yourself

You must take a moment and be compassionate about your situation. This is not the time to blame yourself for having a panic attack. This is the time compassionately validate your reason for having the panic attack. This may sound like this:

"Under my current circumstances and stress levels, it is perfectly acceptable that my body is reacting with a panic attack. I understand that this is the way my body has to react to mentally, emotionally, and physically cope with my current circumstance."

You may also use specifics here. Take the money stress issue from above. This compassionate validation may sound like this:

"Because of my worries about my finances and the pressure of being a provider, it is perfectly acceptable that my body is reacting with a panic attack. I understand that this is the way my body has to react to mentally, emotionally, and physically cope with my current circumstance."

T: Take Action

At this time, you will select a task to do to help your body smoothly move through the emotions and physical symptoms of the panic attack. This step takes some preparation, but I always recommend one technique includes a deep breathing exercise and a mediation. The breathing helps soothe the body because it helps to stabilize the blood pH with oxygenation. This allows the physiological response of the panic attack to normalize gently and rapidly. The meditation helps you connect with your body so that you can develop the acknowledgement and validation for your body's panic attack response. In combination, this breathing and meditation can be executed together. It's best to do the following five steps with your eyes closed. But as you are learning it, feel free to look at the list in between as you perform the following five steps:

Step 1: Identify How You Feel

Take a quick moment to identify your emotion. This does not have to be too detailed. Just simply define a rough estimate of what your mind is doing.

I am stressed
I am angry
I am sad
I am worried

Once you have identified this feeling, that's it! A feeling word is like mad, sad, or glad. An emotion is not a story or description of the situation. This step is deceptively simple, but actually naming an emotion can be hard. Sometimes it helps to have a list of emotions printed out, or you can google something like "list of feeling words." There are lots of lists available online, and all you have to do for this step is pick one that you are feeling in the moment. Don't skip this step. Once you have your emotion identified with a feeling word, move on to step 2.

Step 2: Breathe Deep (The "3-3-3" Breathing Technique)

Plant your feet on the ground with your hands on your lap, or stand in a relaxed stance with hands swinging by your side. Really, any comfortable position will suffice.

Repeat the following breathing technique *three times.*

Breath **in** DEEP for a *count of 3* (feel your <u>gut push out</u> and your <u>back expand</u>)

Hold your breath for a *count of 3* (recall that emotion you identified in Step 1)

Breathe **out** for a *count of 3* (contract your core muscles to exhale; visualize the air leaving the base of your spine and releasing emotion from Step 1)

*In summary: **In** for 3, **hold** for 3, **out** for 3!*

After your three repeats, allow your body to *breathe normally.* At this point, you may feel a little more relaxed. You may feel your temples or heart pulsing a little, or you may feel some calming tingles. You may also feel nothing at all. Breathing can feel so simple that some people skip it, rush it, or jump to self-criticism. Remember we are in the gentle zone, so acknowledge yourself for doing this step. However, you are doing it now is perfect for where you are. Once you have done The "3-3-3" Breathing Technique – however imperfect it feels – move on to the next step.

Step 3: Scan Your Body

The basic task here is to "*scan*" your body with your *attention.* Pay attention to different parts of your body, starting at your feet and moving up towards your head. Place your attention on your feet planted in the ground. Any tension? Wiggle your toes free! Move your attention to your ankles. Any tension? Wiggle free! Now move your attention to your calves. Any tension? Acknowledge them and move up. Repeat this by placing attention to thighs, glutes, groin, pelvic region, abdomen, chest, and back. Pause at the *neck* and *head* and focus a little longer here (we normally hold tons of tension in these areas).

It may help to say *"I release tension here now"* while *exhaling* as you're attending any of your body parts. Once you have scanned your body *to your liking*, move on!

Step 4: Breathe DEEP, Again!

Repeat the "3-3-3" Breathing Technique detailed in Step 2. I know, I know, more breathing! When do we get to the good stuff? But I promise, this is the good stuff. If you want to be able to press stop on your own panic button, then this technique will work. Don't resist it, try it with consistency. Once your blood pH is stabilized, you will have access to new information.

Step 5: Identify How You Feel, Again!

Once again, identify how you *feel* by referring to Step 1 in this process.

After the Technique

You may notice that you have experienced a shift in your mood from when you started. This is great but not required. You may feel buzzing and a decrease in anxiety, or at least a departure from the panic attack. Or you may feel nothing. That's okay too, as long as you don't give up.

This technique takes practice. When I work with my clients, I have them practice this technique three times a day regularly in moments they don't have panic attacks. This allows them to maintain a stable mood and if they do begin to panic, they have practice with the techniques.

The purpose of the A.C.T. Now technique is to quickly move you into a state of allowing. If we resist the panic, push back in any way, it escalates. Remember there are external and internal emotions fueling the panic attack. Allowing dampens the fire. Resisting fuels the fire.

The panic attack is actually a normal physiological response to stress. When we fight that normal bio-logically programmed response, we are increasing the state of distress. This is like trying to put out a fire with gasoline.

The breathing technique and meditation connect you with your body. Your body is not the enemy. Your body is not betraying you with the panic attack. Your body is a neutral tool that is giving you information. The breath work and meditation give you access to that information.

With my clients, they keep a journal with them at all times so they can document their physical, emotional, and mental sensations as soon as the panic is over.

There are a number of other techniques I recommend to my clients as well to help themselves soothe and recover from a panic effectively. This is explored on an individual basis, but some recommendations include:

1. Having a playlist ready with music that make you feel calm or soothed
2. Having a list of friends or family to call that are aware of your tendency to panic that may help you with words of encouragement or in a way you have previously discussed with them.
3. Having an easy access physical activity, like biking or a home workout video, to perform to reduce cortisol levels and increase endorphin levels in the body.

One thing that you may be starting to pick up on is that the panic attack is not *actually* the problem. The panic attack is the response. This technique is the major way for you to start to get in tune with the root cause of the panic.

Repeat after me: *The panic attack is not the problem, it is the response to the problem!*

Panic attacks are actually your body's best way (insufficient as it is) to provide you with critical information that can be used to help identify some kind of dissonance that is existing in your reality. More about identifying the root cause is in chapter 12 of this book, but the A.C.T. Now technique is the first step in identifying the root cause that is particular to you.

As you get used to this idea of being more gentle with yourself, use this technique to help you connect with yourself as often as possible. It will help curb anxiety and panic attacks in progress even before you find the root cause, and it will help build the relationship between you and your body that is required to press stop on your panic button.

There will be many temptations to skip the A.C.T. Now technique. In fact, you might feel like for you, using this technique just isn't something you are physically capable of. Before we can get to the root cause, we have to dismantle the saboteurs of your connection to your own body. We'll get to work on that in the next chapter, so if you were struggling with this step – or maybe read the chapter but didn't practice the technique – keep reading!

CHAPTER 7

BOUNDARY VIOLATIONS CAN CAUSE A PANIC

One of the things that Panickers tend to do in our periods of anxiety and panic is to isolate. Since the great majority of people who panic are also energy-sensitives, this makes sense. Controlling the external emotions seems, logically, to be the best choice. Isolation actually brings about a feeling of safety because it is comfortable and familiar, and there are fewer energy variables to control.

Isolation looks different for different people. For some, isolation may look like locking themselves in their bedroom or apartment. Others socially isolate by keeping their connection circles quite narrow, even in their workplace. Physical energy-sensitives will often avoid specific locations, items, or people.

The isolation, thus, suggest a level of protection is being sought, a sort of defense mechanism.

Because the energy-sensitive is picking up energies from their surroundings, they may become overwhelmed. The emotional energy-sensitive may experience rapid changes in emotions, the physical energy-sensitive may pick up many physical symptoms, and the intuitive may feel like they are losing touch with reality. Isolation behaviors can allow for a moment to let the panic attack symptoms subside in a private location.

In general, the feelings associated with the tendency to isolate are feelings of fear, shame, and anger. The person experiencing the panic is feeling shame about having a panic attack in the first place. They hate that they are experiencing what, to them, feels like loss of control, and they get angry (often at themselves). This panic also brings about an element of fear, especially the first panic, because of the uncertainty element in the nature of the physical symptoms of the panic. The person in a panic attack may even experience their anger as rage, which as I previously discussed, is a cover emotion for more deep emotions.

The isolation really is an attempt to set up a boundary.

What Is a Boundary?

Quite often, boundaries are described as being some sort of "wall" that is put up. It is often some kind of restriction that is directed at a person or external influence. When I was first recognizing boundaries for myself, I didn't have the vocabulary, but I noticed the way I expressed my need or desire for a boundary was to say: "I need my alone time, so give me space."

The problem with this definition of "boundary" is that it externalizes the boundary. It suggests that the person setting the boundary is at the mercy of an external influence of respecting that boundary. If the boundary is an external wall, a lot of time and energy is spent guarding and repairing that wall. Boundaries often get violated quickly because it is tough to watch over the many walls we put up in our environment. As Panickers, we are erecting more and more walls as our panics increase, which gives up more and more guarding and repairing work. That work itself can overwhelm and consume us, creating, yup, you guessed it, *more panic!*

So my definition of "boundary" is different. I still agree we need boundaries, but the way I think it's more productive is if we think of the boundary as simply "self."

A boundary is what makes you YOU and me ME. Not an actual wall. Let me try to explain this with an example. Let's say Jim likes chocolate cake and Sarah likes yellow sponge cake. The boundary is defined by what each respective individual *likes*. The boundary is easily set up here by focusing on knowing what the individual enjoys. If a tray of cupcakes comes out and there are only chocolate cupcakes, Sarah might not choose to have one. Or maybe she will have one even though she knows she won't enjoy it as much as a yellow sponge cake. Her boundary isn't set *against* Jim, it's set *for* herself.

This places the attention on our selves and internalizes the boundary. It maintains itself so long as the focus is placed inward into our own desires. In order for Sarah to set this boundary, all she has to know is what kind of cupcakes she likes. If she *hates* chocolate cupcakes and she eats one anyway, she is violating her own boundary. Now this might sound easy when we talk about cake, but the truth is, most energy-sensitives have been so compromised by external energies, they don't even know what cake they like, never mind the rest of their desires.

In the cake example, notice that those two boundaries are not conflicting. Generally speaking, it doesn't matter if two people, even spouses, have different boundaries about their cake flavor preferences, because those boundaries are rarely a deal breaker.

Boundaries that do conflict sound more like:

Jim likes lots of personal space.

Sarah likes lots of close body contact and intimacy.

These two boundaries conflict.

Or, let's say:

Jim likes personal space and is emotionally triggered when Sarah gets too close. Jim is very likely to describe Sarah as clingy and overly emotional and maybe even demanding.

Sarah, for her part, will say Jim is emotionally unavailable and interprets his behaviors of retreat as "unloving."

I had a client that experienced this exact dynamic. In her situation, she was moved to leave her relationship. Although not all people will be motivated to do such things, her example illustrates how a boundary violation affects panics. Once she left the relationship, her panic attacks stopped – for a while anyway. The root cause of her panic was not the relationship, but the boundary violation had a major button-pressing effect for her.

Remember, there are many energetic exchanges happening among everyone all of the time. The energy-sensitives experience these things on a physical level, really intensely – more intensely than non-energy-sensitive, or energy-typical people. This is why I want to give you permission to be gentle with yourself, you are different than energy-typical people who make up most of the population, that's why this feels so horrible for you and why you think no one understands.

When a boundary violation is constantly occurring, this causes the energy-sensitive to get anxious and reach a state of overwhelm. For an energy-sensitive, it is a normal, predictable, and logical response to all the inputs. You aren't bad, broken, or flawed, you are just energy-sensitive with a set of tools designed for energy-typical people.

This is why isolation for the energy-sensitive is so calming, and why your well-meaning energy-typical friends and family members might be suggesting you are doing too much of it. They just don't have a way to understand.

To an energy-typical person, your isolation may seem like a form of self-sabotage, while for you it's actually an act of self-preservation. The knee-jerk reaction to pull away seems to yield at least some relief and bypasses the need to feel the anger, fear, and shame that accompanies the panic because of social constructs.

How to Develop Stronger Boundaries

"Know thyself" is an ancient Greek aphorism that perfectly illustrates how boundaries are internally defined. In order for energy-sensitives to develop stronger boundaries, it is essential to start to define all of their likes. In other words, simply get to know yourself. Get to know all aspects of yourself, including the food you like, the times of day you like to work, the kinds of people you like to interact with.

With my clients, we set up a "know thyself" binder with tab dividers, whereby each section pertains to a category in which they seek to learn everything about themselves. Some topics are astrology signs, favorite foods, favorite hobbies, a list and image clips of travel destinations of choice, and even favorite crystals.

The binder is a way for them to really connect with themselves and move them into a place of self-awareness, whereby boundaries get established effortlessly.

Another version of this could be done on social media. Pinterest boards can be set up with different topics about yourself and the board filled with all things you LIKE for yourself regarding that topic.

Simply put, the boundary defines our outer limit of our inner world. It is not a wall but rather an acknowledgement of what defines us as whole and complete individuals. A violation of a boundary, whether energetic or otherwise, is a fragmentation of the wholeness we define ourselves as.

It is no wonder that boundaries are a main venue by which the panic attack cascade can be initiated.

Once you have your own "Know Thyself" binder set up online or in physical folders, add to it as much as you can as often as you can. For the first several weeks of working, we are adding to their binder every day to begin separating themselves from the external energies they are so used to syncing with. At this point in your process, action is not required. You don't need to quit your job, or file for divorce, or give up your dream. You just need to observe. If you struggle with this, as many of my clients do, or if you want to go faster, you want to consider working with a life coach. I will say when I was doing this work, it was very hard for me, but as a trained scientist, I am good at looking for and recording evidence. I didn't have a coach at the time, but I was very committed to my own growth and watched videos and read books almost every minute I wasn't at work. Honestly, had I run into a coach or a program that solved it in my words I would have said "*Take my money*" instantly, but I didn't know such things existed, so I took the longer, slower, DIY route myself.

One of my first boundaries that I identified was that I personally needed sleep. This wasn't a boundary I was setting against my job, or my friends, or my family. It was just that I, Ramses, needed six hours of sleep per night, less than most, more than some – but that's what I know about me. In order to not violate my own boundaries, I had to find a way to get that every night, without exception. In the next chapter, I'll show you how I did it, and why the first thing you want to work on from your "Know Thyself" binder are your physical needs. Until your physical needs, like sleep, are met, you won't have the reserves to get to the root cause of your panics. The next few steps will help us peel back the onion and get to the root cause, which we will tackle in chapter 12. Don't skip ahead!

CHAPTER 8

HOW SLEEP CONTRIBUTES TO STABILITY

Like many other aspects of your health, being panic attack free comes down to lifestyle choices. There is no magic pharmaceutical drug that can or will solve your panic attack problems. Lots of people will get rich selling you solutions to the symptoms, but when it comes to panic attacks, the results will be temporary and disappointing. Some drugs may relieve some symptoms some of the time, but without addressing the root cause, you will not be able to press stop on your panic button. To get to that root cause, energy-sensitives must take special care to make lifestyle choices that minimize the chances of their anxiety from creeping up. In this chapter, we will review some of those basic self-care tools that are the lifestyle choices required to end your panic forever.

Sleep is critical for energy-sensitives because sleep from the night before can determine large portions of the next day. The energy and anxiety that we experience in the morning bleeds over from the night before. All of the thoughts and anxiety from the previous day affect how we sleep, and thus how we wake up and start the day.

Before we get into the sleep, this is probably a very good time to explain the concept of the Law of Attraction.

I first heard about this law when my mother sent me the book *The Secret* by Rhonda Byrne. Although the focus of the book was irrelevant to me at the time, understanding the science behind the Law of Attraction became a mild curiosity for me. The Law of Attraction had stated that we were attracting into our reality those things that we are focused on. Me being the science-y brain that I am could not just take something like this at face value. I had to understand *how* this could actually be true! Remember when I quoted Tesla, that everything is energy, frequency, and vibration? I wondered if this was the vehicle by which the Law of Attraction worked. If like energies are present, they have the ability to vibrationally add up. So, if we focus on positive, we can "add" positive to our reality!

If we focus on negative, well, the opposite also holds true.

When it comes to sleep, for instance, setting up your sleep "vibes" are important for attracting better feeling moods and emotions while sleeping which thus gives you a running start on curbing anxiety and panic the next day.

To do this, it is important that energy-sensitives set up nighttime and morning time routines. With my clients, I help them tailor their routines in the most comfortable way for their lifestyle. For example, your routine may have to revolve around work, exercise, children, spouses, and living conditions. Here are some of the key features I help my clients customize to make sure they are setting up the best possible morning.

Going to Sleep

Your nighttime routine should contain three main ingredients:

1. A way to decompress from the day
2. A way to soothe yourself
3. A way to elevate your emotional vibration

These three items are so intimately related that its almost tough to tease them apart, but including these items are key to setting up our vibration for the upcoming day. Decompressing may look like having a cup of your favorite relaxing tea at the beginning of your routine. You want to be able to sit and let your mind completely run its thoughts without interruption or judgment.

Soothing is necessary to set up a feeling of safety in your body. Remember, much of the reason your body is in constant anxiety (with panic attack spikes) is that the external energies around you combine that with your internal energy, also called your vibration, and it makes sense that your nervous system can go on the fritz! The fight-or-flight mechanism is constantly activated, which is your body's way of standing on guard because of impending doom or danger. Finding a way to soothe your nervous system allows for you to get into a point to raise your vibration.

When I did my "Know Thyself" binder, I discovered that I generally require more relaxation than sleep. So I take salt water baths before bed. Sometimes I include tea tree, mint, and lavender essential oil to the bath to add to the feeling of soothing, relaxation, and comfort. This step may seem like a luxury, but for the constant Panicker, this is a necessary step to allow for the nervous systems to calm down and ease into sleep.

Elevating your vibration is essential to set up your sleep state. You can go to bed after just relaxing, but if you take an additional step to go to bed feeling better emotionally, you will wake up in a better headspace. Unfortunately, for those of us who have suffered from panic, this is a new skill you will have to learn. Think of it this way: You've spent ten, twenty, maybe thirty years teaching yourself to be really good at panicking before bed, now you have a new skill to learn – how to soothe yourself before bed. It may feel effortful to feel better when we are accustomed to worrying and sitting in states of fear, anger, sadness, and general upset, but that's only because it's new. After all, if worrying was working for you, you wouldn't be reading this book!

One of the ways my clients like to raise their emotional vibration before bed is doing a gratitude list right before falling asleep. To try this step, keep a journal by your bed. After you are tucked in, fill one entire page with a list of things you are grateful for in your surroundings. The list may include how comfy your bed and pillows are, how beautiful the color of your room is to you, or the wonderful feeling of your skin after an essential oils bath. After this list is complete, allow yourself to fall asleep while repeating or continuing this list in your head.

Note that there is no mention of watching television or being on your mobile devices here. There is also no mention of distracting yourself from emotions by reading. These tasks can be done before the decompression phase for your night routine, but should not be included in your nighttime ritual. If you distract and keep the low vibrational thoughts and emotions inside of you, you will attract more of the same as you fall asleep, while sleeping, and subsequently, when you wake up. These three steps are set up to *allow* yourself to rest and to let go of the vibrations that keep your nervous system in alert or fight-or-flight mode.

Waking Up

My client Kristy described waking up to me as being peaceful at first, a state of calm and bliss while she is in the "weird transition phase between sleep and wakefulness." She then described how she would experience anxiety as she became more consciously aware of being awake from sleep.

There are three steps to a morning time ritual that will capitalize on the work set up prior to going to bed, and also help you propel yourself into your day with an active and positive vibe. The three steps are as follows:

1. Decompress
2. Elevate your vibration
3. Engage your energy

Notice that this is almost the reverse of your nighttime routine. And for good reason! Many energy-sensitives have very lucid dreams or have many extrasensory events occur to them as they sleep. Decompressing from all of these events may be necessary to start to process the day. I recommend keeping a dream journal right by the bed or in your night stand, ready for you when you wake up. In that journal document, all the dreams and thoughts that you have so that you can have room to move into elevating your vibration. We want to identify your exact emotional and energetic starting point of the day. If nothing is on your mind right when you wake up, move into the next step of raising your vibration. If something happened in the night, don't ignore it or push it away, acknowledge it in your dream journal. Only when you are decompressed should you move on to elevate your vibration. This step can't be forced and still work, so wake up early enough to give yourself ten-twenty minutes to decompress if you need it.

When you are ready, turn your attention to elevating your vibration. Mindfulness or point meditations, like candle gazing meditations, work well here, or you may want to create another gratitude list or a positive affirmations list here. Positive affirmations are very useful to perform only if done correctly. Often times people are told to look themselves in the mirror and tell themselves "I love you." The problem is, if you don't believe that, saying this is an assault to your intelligence. You must say positive affirmations that are realistic to your situation and current energetic feeling. I suggest stating your emotions out loud and then saying something that feels a little bit better than your current feeling. Saying "I love you" to yourself may feel like too big of an emotional leap to say if you are feeling upset. But saying "I'm glad you woke up and are attempting to have a good day" may feel more realistic and may feel better to say than "I love you." Write a page in a positive affirmations journal with only items that feel real and true for you based on your current vibrations. This helps you systematically "inch up" the emotional scale and thus releases you from attracting negative vibes early in the day.

It is important to help your body process stress hormones and to increase endorphins that help you remain in a feeling state of soothing, clarity, and comfort. In the next chapter, I will discuss diet in more detail, but eating a breakfast that allows for your body to start working and remain calm are an essential part of waking up. To relieve stress hormones and to add endorphins, going to the gym, going for a walk, or even incorporating a stretching or yoga routine for fifteen-minutes works well here to engage your energy.

It is essential that the energy-sensitive realize that there is great strength in setting up our energetics around going to sleep and waking up from sleep. Rest is essential for our nervous systems that are constantly consciously processing information. Naps may even be in order for some sensitives. You get a running start on your energy when you approach rest and waking with routines and awareness.

CHAPTER 9

FOODS AFFECT YOUR MOODS

Food is especially important for the energy-sensitive. There are many different diet types that one could adopt for themselves, but here I want to focus primarily on something simpler than a diet plan, and that is our relationship with food.

The truth is that we must develop a relationship with the foods we eat in a way that is beneficial to our sensitivities. The most important question to ask at this point is "what exactly is a relationship with food?"

The reason this is important to address is because it is so simple. We often don't even consider the interaction we have with food do be an actual "relationship." But in fact, we are in a very intimate relationship with food, and often our dysfunctions with food affect our reality more than we realize. Energy-sensitives must understand, develop, and cultivate this relationship over time in order to maximize their vibration.

To do this, start by asking questions to yourself about your food, such as:

- What foods do I like?
- What foods do I crave?
- What foods do I hate and why?
- Do I like savory or sweet foods more?
- Do I like anything bitter?
- Do I prefer eating at a certain time of day? What are those times?
- Do I eat late at night? Why?
- Do I fantasize about food?
- Do I hate the idea of people looking at me eat?
- Do I like to eat alone?
- Do I like to cook? Under what conditions?
- Do I eat when I am emotional?
- How does the food feel inside me?

These are just a few of the components that are involved in your relationship with food. Food is so much more than nutrients for our body's physical survival. You have a relationship with food already – everyone does. Do you like that relationship? If not, now is the time to work on it!

Emotional Eating

Many energy-sensitives do participate in some form of emotional eating. This can range from eating chocolate when sad and alone at home to full blown eating disorders centered around your own emotional states.

I am a recovering bulimic. When I was in college, I remember this panicky feeling I would get after a long day. I just wanted to go to the supermarket and buy lots of cheap food so that I could just lose myself in a binge. I was also self-conscious about being overweight so I would purge with Magnesium Citrate laxatives. Binging and purging took me to a numbing trance-like state which was at once terrible and also sort of soothing.

Looking back, I can see how I craved this quasi-soothing state for one simple reason – I had something to be soothed from. This meant that there was some emotion that was not soothing. There were a whole lot of emotions that I would cover up when I overate. The anxiety momentarily was gone while I got high off the happy chemicals released in my brain from a binge. The moment that I was able to address the emotions directly was the moment I was able to release the anxiety that led to my binging and purging cycle.

Negative Food Relationships Have a Purpose

My body fat and eating disorder served me. I was overweight because I didn't want to feel my feelings, and the extra fat had an insulating effect shielding me from external energies coming through. It worked in some ways. The more overweight I felt, the more I would isolate, thereby minimizing the number of external energies I was exposed to.

The moment I realized my fat was serving a purpose in my life, was the moment that I really started to gain control of my weight. I was able to directly do things that helped manage my external energy intake and thus relieved myself of the need for my body fat.

My eating disorder also had a purpose. After a long day of not having energy filters, my anxiety and nervous system wanted a little break. I would go into a binge trance and escape my reality. Although this may be a triggering thought for some, it amazes me to this day that my eating disorder actually was sticking around to help me. This realization about my weight and my eating disorder allowed me to forgive myself and create a new relationship with food.

Correcting the Aftermath with Mindful Eating

Although my fat and eating disorder had many positives for me, I was ready to let them go. For starters, my GI took a hit with all of the laxative purges I put it through. I developed really volatile Irritable Bowel Syndrome. I had to be hyper vigilant about what foods

I ate. Too much fiber or too little caused drastic changes in my "style of going," and adding these concerns to my many food intolerances including dairy, some nuts, and some grains, was getting complicated.

There were a number of things I learned from my unhealthy food relationship that helped me not only lose weight, but also to gain control of my sensitivities.

What I learned, I was surprised to find out, is actually called mindful eating. Now, when I eat, I make it a habit to eat while doing nothing else. I put food in my mouth and I feel how it feels as I chew. I take the time to taste all the flavors in the food. When I swallow the bolus of food, I feel how it feels as it travels down my throat and into my stomach. After completing my meal, I feel the sensations in my GI. I allow myself to sink into the feeling of satiation and of fulfillment. This allows my brain to register that I am full and no longer need food at the moment. I let it sit in me with gratitude. Through the day, I check in with my gut to see how it feels. I sit quietly and place my hands over my belly and give my digestion some attention. I determine if I feel any discomfort or pain. Then I relate the feeling to the foods I ate to see if there is any cause for any discomfort I may be feeling.

I do this with every meal or snack I eat. I realized

that my GI likes to digest foods differently at night than it does in the morning. So I adjust my food intake to accommodate for those fluctuations in digestive rates and efficacies I experience throughout the day.

I teach my clients meditations for mindful eating so that they can learn for themselves what kinds of foods to eat and when. If you aren't working with a coach on this, make sure you take great notes on exactly what you are eating and when to see what works for you. It's very personal.

General Food Tips for the Energy-Sensitive

There are many factors about food that can affect your internal energy and your ability to feel stable in your surroundings. To avoid getting into states of panic, the most basic thing I suggest to my clients is to make sure that their blood glucose level is stabilized through the day. There is almost a "buzzy" feeling and irritability that comes from the glucose dip. Finding out what foods help with this stability is important.

Personally, I eat a plant-based diet. Not only did this switch alleviate many of my IBS symptoms, it also allowed me to feel less emotionally-charged. I realized that part of my emotions were set off by the energy residues existing in the animal meat I was consuming.

I would have feelings of trauma surrounding my food, so I opted to cut them out of my diet. Not surprisingly, my emotions around food stabilized drastically. My clients that are food energy-sensitives have reported this to me as well.

Food also sets up your day. I found that If I ate foods that made me jittery, like coffee, I would feel more of an anxiety roller coaster through the day. Also, if I didn't eat, this would also happen.

As energy-sensitives, the food we eat can have a dramatic effect on our anxiety levels. Mindful eating is the best tool to learn what food combinations will work for you. No externally-directed diet plan can ever do that for you, and in fact eating a diet plan recommended to you – even by an expert – can cause an increase in your anxiety and panics.

CHAPTER 10

RELATIONSHIP REALITIES ARE A BIG DEAL!

Contrast is everywhere. We experience darkness by virtue of experiencing light, we know what "up" is because we know what "down" is, and the list goes on from here. One of the best ways to experience contrast is through relationships. Relationships highlight the best and the worst between all the parties involved. This includes professional relationships, friendship relationships, and, of course, romantic relationships. We automatically know what we do like in relationships, but when there is something we don't like in our interactions, it is an opportunity to pay attention to how we are feeling. There is that seed of gentle curiosity coming through again.

Consider my client, Mat. Before he came to work with me, Mat had been in a relationship with a narcissist. After the relationship ended, he felt stuck making mental lists of all the things that, as he called it, "pissed" him off about his ex-boyfriend. When he came to me, Mat's speech was peppered with phrases like:

"I hate that he always lied to me."

"I hate that he always made me feel like my reaction to his actions were wrong."

"I hate that he never wanted to commit to the relationship."

"I hate that he never had time to listen to MY problems."

"I hate that I always had to perform certain sexual activities with him in a way that pleases him."

"I hate that I had to always go to his house to interact with him, and that he was unwilling to be seen in a relationship with me."

After some time of venting, I remember asking Mat, "Is there at all a benefit to the list you just told me? Does this list reveal anything important for you that you *actually* use to feel better?"

Right away he answered, "No. Absolutely not."

I invited him to consider it more.

After some thought, he confirmed. He still had nothing.

To my amazement, Mat was unable to see that all of those experiences were actually points of contrast. I told him, "Mat, I want you to take this list and consider the *preferred* outcome for each statement. Also, reword it positively. Does it feel better or worse to think?"

So, he did this. The statement, "I hate that he always lied to me" turned into "I want him to always be honest with me." The idea, "I hate that he never had time to listen to *my* problems" became "I want him to listen to my problems." And so on the list went.

Mat, without meaning to, had created the perfect list of qualities he needed for his next partner. Now if I had just asked Mat, "What do you want in a partner?" he probably wouldn't have been able to answer me. After all, we hadn't even gotten to his "Know Thyself" binder yet. But he had his list of preferences already. By virtue of the "points of contrast" in that previous relationship, he now had the exact map to navigate towards a romantic relationship that made him feel satisfied and safe.

Because of the amount of information that we attain from the relationships, it is no wonder why they are so important for us to focus on.

There are three major relationship interactions that exist in relationships that can create anxiety. Energy-typical and energy-sensitives participate in each of these interactions quite differently. For energy-sensitives, this relationship anxiety can lead to panic and ultimately full-on panic attacks.

Your job as you read about these types is to think of examples where you have had your personal boundaries crossed because you didn't understand your preferences and needs. Your list will help you to create your own list of needs and preferences, much like Mat did.

Three Relationship Interactions That Can Set off a Panic

GASLIGHTING

Gaslighting is the direct rejection of an individual's experience. In other words, a gaslighting experience is when someone says, "What you see, you didn't see; what you heard, you didn't hear; what you felt, you didn't feel."

If you are energy-typical, gaslighting might be a tad bit annoying, but you will simply know in your heart this isn't true and move on. Maybe you will confront the person, maybe you won't; but you won't be confused about what your truth is.

For an energy-sensitive, however, it's a frighteningly different story. Energy-sensitives are often at the mercy of gaslighting experiences because their boundaries are not clear. Remember, my definition a boundary is "knowing yourself." When the energy-sensitive is unclear of the energy they are perceiving, as in emotional energy, they can quite easily fall victim to over-empathizing in their relationships and thus neglect trusting themselves. In a later chapter I will discuss how this self-distrust is rooted in subconscious trauma, but for now, suffice to say that the lack of self-trust by the energy-sensitive results in abuse by gaslighting.

In Mat's case, his narcissistic ex would say certain abusive comments to him and then later deny saying such things altogether. After enough iterations of this behavior, Mat began to doubt his own sanity and perceptive reality. This put Mat in a position to be easily manipulated by his ex. When Mat came to see me, we spent much of the time helping him develop his own personal boundaries in a way that helped him focus positively on the aspects he required in a relationship instead.

BYPASSING

Bypassing is another situation that sets off the energy-sensitive who panics. Bypassing is an avoidance tactic where someone uses religion, science, or spirituality to "go around," or "bypass," a situation that needs direct attention.

Why does this set off the energy-sensitive in panic mode? Well remember, energy-sensitives in general always pick up on the "elephant in the room" no matter how small the elephant is. Because of their highly-developed sensitivity, they usually pick up on *all* the elephants in the room regarding all parties present and sometimes even those present in spirit or animal form. Energy typical people can find it hard to imagine how triggering it can be to know there is a ton of negative energy in the room even though what's being showcased is all smiles. For an energy-sensitive, however, this is a sadly too common occurrence, with no one to share it.

One time, I was at a gathering of supposedly "Spiritually-Enlightened" people. Everyone was all smiles. I hugged a perfect stranger in a bright yellow sweater and as I pulled her close the smell of Jasmine and Patchouli essential oil lifted into the air! She was so "put together!" I can't remember our conversation now, but I wanted to be real and deep and she just kept spinning phrases like "everything is love and is happening because it is supposed to be happening," or "everything happens for a reason." I just wasn't buying it. I wanted to like her but I knew – somehow I just knew – she was in a dark place and we weren't really connecting. I was meeting a character-actor and not a real person.

Sunny McSunshine was modeling spiritual bypassing. She was "bypassing" how she truly felt and inauthentically showcasing positivity.

This is not the only way that bypassing shows up. People bypass by being overly positive, when they hyper intellectualize to logic their way into staying in abusive relationships. I've even had a client whose family used religious quotes and bible passages to suppress and repress their true emotional states.

To the energy-sensitive, this situation invokes distrust. The energy-sensitive can feel into the bypass-er's true state and thus "calls the bluff" internally. This registers as a "fake" person instantly and becomes an individual that should not be trusted. Unfortunately, few energy-sensitives call out the situation because to do so creates panic. Instead, the energy-sensitive commonly retreats and they begin to develop intense distrust in the world-at-large. When an energy-sensitive does confront someone on the dissonance, very often the person confronted will say "What are you talking about? This is all in your head!" And thus, the energy-sensitive is gaslighted once more.

For the energy-sensitive, encountering "bypassers" constantly leads to a condition where they are unable to trust people whether they confront them or stay silent.

The remedy to bypassing is authenticity. Speaking your truth is only one piece of the answer. You must also practice staying in your truth. I recommend stating your emotions as they come up and not lessening your emotional experiences when referring to your life. I often tell the story of me watching Disney movies, especially the movie *The Lion King*. I sob every time when Mufasa dies. My heart melts. Practicing stating your emotion is a way of building up the skills of both speaking your truth and standing in your power. As an energy-sensitive who panics, this is almost certainly a skill you have not yet fully developed. Fear not though, it is very learnable!

When you master this, you will have a sense of clarity and power. You won't feel insane or gaslighted in situations like these any longer.

DUMPING

As you know, energy-sensitives are able to feel the effects of emotions around them. Often these emotions make their nervous systems start to panic. Among energy-typicals, this doesn't happen. So let's just say you are quietly minding your own business at your co-working office and head over to the coffee machine for a cup between chapters of your forthcoming book. At the coffee machine, you see someone you have met before in this space. Immediately, as you are waiting for the pod machine to produce your java, this near-stranger has dumped all of her emotional baggage on you without regard to what it is doing to your emotional state. The co-working space over-billed her. "Did they overbill you too?" This led to several checks bounding this month and now the co-working space wants to keep the fee for next month but she can't make her rent for this month. Plus, her kid wants ice skating lessons! How is she supposed to come up with $200 a month for lessons and new skates with this going down? She and her husband are fighting. She wants to borrow money from her mom to close the gap. What do you think?

If you are like most energy-sensitives, what you think is that you want your coffee and headphones back on!

Would you believe energy-typicals think this is small talk?! They just smile and let it roll on by. To an energy-sensitive, I don't have to tell you that this dumping feels draining to say the least.

Why is this the case? Because energy-sensitives are hyper-aware of the energies that match their current emotional state. Remember those mirror-neurons I had my client Nicoal read about? That's what's happening with you. Maybe you have a bill you haven't paid, and you have some stress about that. Well not only are you listening to this strangers' bill problems but all of the emotions around your unpaid bills are also being triggered by those mirror neurons.

Once you understand this is your unique biology and not some personal failing or weakness, it's easier to create a boundary. The truth is, dumping doesn't work for you. You don't need to explain this, but you need to be responsible for managing your own energy and in the case of the "dumping," co-worker you might say something like:

"Ugh! I can see that you are having a tough time. I hate to cut you off, but I am on deadline and I really need to use every ounce of my energy to complete my work tasks at the moment. Can we chat about this another time?"

You can get as creative with this as possible, but it is important to convey that your internal boundary of feeling calm and focused with your own priorities are expressed.

Two Relationship Dynamics That Set off Panics in the Energy-Sensitive

There are two additional relationship dynamics that can be particularly draining to energy-sensitives.

The first is the energy vampire. Energy vampires are masters of dumping, but they gravitate to dumping specifically on energy-sensitives because of our heightened perceived sense of empathy. They may not only dump on you, but may also be highly interruptive in conversation in both social/professional settings and in simple conversation. Energy vampires are the people with whom it's tough to "get a word in edgewise." The energy vampire experience is a relative one. Someone might be an energy vampire for you, but that same person might be a delight for another energy-sensitive. Not only that, but energy vampires can be energy-typical or energy-sensitive themselves! The only way to manage someone who is an energy vampire for you is to first recognize that the person IS an energy vampire for you and limit your interaction, full stop. Yes, even if it's your mom.

The second relationship dynamic that is particularly dangerous for the energy-sensitive is the narcissist. The narcissist dynamic centers around the behaviors set up by a system of intermittent rewards. This is exactly what makes gambling addictive for some people. There is a push and pull dynamic between the energy-sensitive and the narcissist which feeds the brain with neurotransmitters that signal to keep playing the game. The narcissist is unable to empathize with the sensitive while the sensitive overly empathizes with the narcissist. For energy-sensitives, this creates a completely unsustainable and wholly draining relationship.

Like energy vampires, relationships with narcissists are a hard-no for energy-sensitives.

Relationships between a narcissist and an energy-sensitive are fueled by the internal and often subconscious pain and trauma from the past. The narcissist might have been abandoned as a child, with no validation for their emotions. The narcissist then creates a coping method where they think: "I must always depend on myself for everything. I must figure everything out for myself." In reality, intimacy does not feel safe to them because it triggers the feeling of abandonment they have felt in the past when the parent rejected and denied them.

The energy-sensitive may have felt similar abandonment as a child, but the coping method they created was to seek deeper, yet unfulfilling intimacy. The need for each in this dynamic is the trigger for the other. The closer the energy-sensitive moves towards the narcissist, the more the narcissist retreats. The more the narcissist retreats, the more isolated the energy-sensitive feels. Deep down inside, the narcissist does want intimacy. The narcissist wants to figure everything out for him or herself. But they show intimacy (the thing the energy-sensitive most desires) sparingly and randomly, thus keep the energy-sensitive "addicted" though the intermittent reward phenomenon.

Ironically, like energy vampires, narcissists can also be energy-sensitive. In fact, narcissists may actually be SO hypersensitive, in a subconscious way, that they end up evading all other encounters that don't meet the surface level needs they are conscious about. In other words, they could actually be the *ultimate* form of energy-sensitives.

The "problem" with narcissists is that they never see a real motive to be intimate. All the evidence they have acquired in their reality supports the belief "I can do this on my own."

In short, steer clear energy-sensitive one – this is not a game you will be rewarded for playing. I know of that which I speak.

While energy-sensitives must avoid or minimize exposure to energy vampires and narcissists, they must learn to manage and set boundaries around more normal energy-typical interactions like gaslighting, bypassing, and dumping. Your first job is to recognize and catalog these three interaction types and two dynamics. How do they show up in your world? Sometimes spotting it can be ninety percent of the challenge. Once you spot these experiences and name them, you will need to work with a coach or on your own to customize your own game-plan for dealing with these situations. Remember, relationships in general are there to provide contrast. What works for you, works for you. When something isn't working, you are just gathering more clues and information about what you need in the relationships that fill your world.

CHAPTER 11

LISTENING TO YOUR INNER VOICE

Intuition is your inner voice. Newsflash, my energy-sensitive friend, the intuition force is strong with us. We energy-sensitives must pay particular attention to our intuition. Your failure to connect with your inner voice and to understand what it is saying will – for sure – lead to panic attacks, and possibly other physical and mental health issues, too. Your inner voice will find a way to communicate with you come hell or high water.

For my science-loving compadres, I know this may still seem a little too esoteric for you. Intuition? Inner voice? What does that mean anyway? Let me give it to you in straight scientific terms. Your inner voice is simply the binary, positive or negative charge you have to any external stimulus. You, my friend, are a magnet. You will be pulled toward or away from things and that pulling toward or away from feeling – that's your intuition.

Ever been walking down an ally or hallway and get a feeling of impending doom? That is generally your intuition giving you information. The feeling may be negative, not necessarily because something bad is happening to you, but because you, somehow, PERCIEVE something negative in your reality. It is important to realize that your intuition is never wrong for you in the moment you connect with it. It is, however, highly limited to the current perspectives in your reality.

Your brain can only know what it knows, consciously, so the information your intuition provides has limitations. For this reason, we must learn to find out how our inner voice communicates with us, because the voice is always speaking the most "correct" answer for us at that time.

It is important for the energy-sensitive to honor the intuition, or to gently and compassionately question it. When we don't honor our intuition, or worse when we attack it, we develop a sense of distrust with ourselves, which, you guessed it, leads to panic. Not listening to your inner voice is an expression of self-abandonment. It feels like yourself, telling yourself, that you don't trust you to make good decisions. Your relationship with yourself is the most important one you will ever have, and not listening to your intuition is a deal-breaker for that relationship. Since your inner voice can't suggest you go to couples counselling, it throws a panic attack to get your attention.

When we ignore our inner voice, we become the bypasser, and in some cases, even the gaslighter to ourselves. We must also be aware of how others' actions and pressures put us in situations where we may feel like it is not conducive for us to trust our intuition.

Take group outings for instance. Say your whole writer's group is going to a bar for happy hour, and intuitively you have a negative pull about this idea, but you are worried that it would be somehow not be okay to obey your inner voice. *Don't go!*

I can *not* say this loudly or clearly enough. You must always, always, always trust your inner voice. Denying it will make you feel bulldozed and is a set up for emotional abuse within the group and even self-abuse by you, to you.

My father shared with me a very interesting anecdote from his youth. At the time, he was still living in Puerto Rico. He and his friends were at a local dance hot spot where everyone was drinking, dancing, and over all just having a good time. Suddenly, he felt the urge to leave! His friends did not understand his seemingly impulsive reaction. One other friend decided to join him. Later that week, he found out that the chair that he was sitting on had gotten shot by a stray bullet from a neighboring hunting zone. His decision to leave was right for him and only him!

When we trust our intuition, we offer ourselves a feeling of surety and security. We become the drivers of our own vehicle. This allows us to attract more surety, confidence, stillness, clarity and calmness.

We can connect to our intuition a number of ways. I'm going to outline a two of my and my client's favorite ways here.

Connecting to Intuition Through Meditation

Meditation offers up some of the most clear from of intuition communication. It is important that you relax yourself before you begin to "check in" with your inner voice. I always teach my clients to start every meditation by observing the breath. For this reason, always check in with your voice after performing the 3-3-3 breathing technique that I offer up in chapter 6.

The breathing allows you to become present to yourself. Remember to bring your attention to your internal reality as you observe your breath. At that moment, you can internally (or out loud) ask your intuition a question to which you are seeking an answer. Ask questions in a binary form, meaning the answer can be easily be interpreted as a "yes" or "no." A question like "should I have fish sticks for dinner?" will yield a clear yes or no answer. An answer to a question like "what should I have for dinner?" will not be as clear, especially as you are building your relationship with yourself.

A "yes" response from your intuition will feel like a brightening, energizing feeling. It may feel like tingling or like a light is originating from your gut region. A "no" response will feel like a dulling or negative emotion. It may feel like a "gut punch" sensation or a binding "shackles on" feeling. Any negative feeling suggests a "no" response.

When you ask questions that don't naturally yield a yes or no answer, you may get a vision or thought that has to be interpreted in order to get an answer. Alternatively, you may experience synchronicities in your reality that reveal the answer. Synchronicities are events that line up with your focused thought. Take the open-ended question, "What should I have for dinner tonight?" You may see commercials about fish, you may notice a fish restaurant on the way home from an errand, or you may even hear a child on the street make a request for fish sticks! Look for synchronicities and you will get an answer if you are paying attention.

Using Divination to Connect with Your Inner Voice

Divination modalities are just tools a person can use to communicate with their own intuition. Divination tools include things like tarot cards, pendulums, Ouija boards, tea leaves, crystal balls, and rune tiles. To be honest, divination scared me at first. My science-trained brained felt like it was too "woo-woo" for me. So, I put them to the test like any well-trained scientist. The list of divination tools is practically endless, but no matter what I tried, the effect was always the same, I gained some clarity about what was right for me. I connected with my intuition. Woo-woo or not, I proved to myself these tools worked for me.

In my opinion, the divination tools helped me bypass my conscious, often anxious, mind. For me, it's a way of going around a distracting thought or to approach difficult question without being biased by my own emotion in the moment. Divination tools help me gain clarity – especially in situations are more "dense" with potential biases. Also, not gonna lie, divination tools could simply just not be more fun!

However you do it, on your own or with a coach, in

order to press stop on your panic button, you are going to have to learn your own favorite ways to connect with your intuition. Start with these, but stay open. Your inner voice is always talking. At the beginning it's just a whisper, but if you don't listen early, it will become a scream that often sounds like a panic attack. The better your relationship with yourself is, the earlier you will be able to hear your intuition so you no longer have to wait until it becomes that unbearable noise that only a Panicker knows and dreads.

CHAPTER 12

NO LIMITS TO YOUR CURE

At the beginning of this book, I promised you that we could press stop on your panic and that to do that we had to get to the root cause. To get to the root cause and address it, you will need the tool box we have reviewed in the last several chapters. You will need the A.C.T. Now method to catch your panics in progress and slow or stop them. You will need to get to know yourself and your preferences and practice setting boundaries that support those needs. You will need to develop lifestyle choices around sleep and food that support your relationship with yourself. You will need to cultivate relationships that support you and to release those that don't. And if you do that, you will create a magical space to deepen your connection to your own GPS system – your intuition.

If you are one of those people who like to jump ahead to the conclusion, I should warn you now, knowing the root cause of your panic attacks is the only way to cure them, but the information in this chapter alone is not enough. In fact, if you haven't read the last chapters and you read this now, your brain will likely dismiss it as an insufficient explanation. I promise, it's not. The ground must be tilled before the seeds are planted.

Most panic attacks are never cured because almost every cure on its own usually solves some symptoms while creating others. The panics are often the thing that is being treated when in fact, the panics themselves are not the problem. I still remember the moment I realized there was more to my panics than just the symptoms. I went into work that day panicking and left work eight hours later still panicking. My symptoms were being managed by the medicine I was on, and the complementary techniques I'd started to learn – like meditation, energy healing, crystal therapy, aroma therapy, and sound therapy – were starting to make an impact. In addition to the pharmaceutical approach, I had systematically implemented subconscious regression meditation, mindfulness mediations, I became a master Reiki practitioner doing self-healing sessions, I changed my diet, and worked with a relationship coach who helped me see that it was time to let go of my toxic relationships.

That night after work, I made myself a soothing cup of chamomile tea and drew a salt and lavender bath. As I took my last sip of tea, I had this spark of an idea that, maybe, just maybe, I knew the reason for my panics. I slipped off my robe and stepped carefully into the tub, fully submerging my body, and my head felt soft and warm and calm and comforting. As I came up for air, the answer was fully formed in my mind: *My panic attacks were designed to tell me that I was not doing what I was meant to be doing with my life.*

I was working a nine-to-five laboratory job as a research and development scientist for a cancer institute, a job that I thought I wanted, but I was panicking throughout my whole stay there.

I was also in a relationship with an abusive narcissist, and I was being gaslighted and bypassed constantly at work, in my relationship, and worst of all, by myself. My boundaries were being violated constantly.

The panic attacks were my way of getting my own attention. They were screaming: *This life is not serving you! Change everything now!*

And for my part... I wasn't listening. I was meditating and medicating and all the while ignoring the message my inner voice was trying to get to me. Today, I am grateful to my inner voice for not giving up on me.

It turns out the panic attacks weren't even a problem.

They were not the thing that needed to be cured. They weren't the enemy. In fact, I quickly began to realize that the panic attacks were just neutral information I was making available to myself. They were the clear set of alarms telling me to make adjustments to my life. The panics told me that I was in a place that I had to let go of things in my life that no longer served me.

In fact (and I know if you skipped ahead that this is going to sound like complete nonsense), I actually came to love how panic attacks were really on my side all along. There was nothing wrong with them. Taking the medications was like hitting the snooze button on the panics, and for good reason. If I stifled them forever, I would never have gotten to the point where I realized all of my sensitivities and the advantage they give me.

My energetic sensitivities are now something that I am happy I have. They allow me to navigate my world with clarity, to read people, and to help the authors I work with at The Author Incubator at a more intimate level. The very thing that *caused* my panic attacks is actually my superpower. As Maya Angelou says, "I wouldn't take nothing for my journey now."

I remember a client telling me about his past in a narcissistic relationship.

I told him, "I bet you felt like he was shaming you

and that somehow your point of view was not important. He probably made you second guess yourself and you probably feel like you're overreacting. You feel like crying now don't you. You feel like a density is being cleared from you field of vision. You feel your throat tightening up right now."

He said, "Holy crap! How did you know all that?"

That's my superpower. I can feel everything around me. And I can turn it down to protect my own boundaries, too. How could I ever turn my back on that gift?

What I know for sure is that we can really live a life of being panic free, because the truth is, we always have. Panics are not, and never will be the problem. The dissonance in our lives are what need to be addressed.

Earlier I asked, *are panic attacks killing your dreams?*

Truth time: That was a trick question. Your panic attacks are pointing the way to your dreams. They are illuminating the path so you can clear it. Your anxiety is telling you everything you need to know to have everything you ever wanted.

Are you ready to listen?

CONCLUSION

THE MAGIC PILL

I was running out of options for what to try to cure myself of panic attacks. Meditation didn't work. Medications didn't work. My job was at risk and my dreams had been suffocated. As a scientist, it was hard for me to keep an open mind about all of this, but the alternative of sticking with the doctor-prescribed approach just wasn't working.

I explored as many options as possible in order to find what worked for me. I became curious about energy healing when I learned I was an energy-sensitive. I wanted to know if I could gain better understanding of what energy flowing in and out of me felt like. That was the scientist in me talking! I really wanted to feel energy flowing in order for me to believe that it was possible for me to be exchanging energy with my surroundings.

I decided to try Reiki Energy Healing because I wanted to validate my theories of energy exchange as an "empath." As an emotional intuitive empath, I had no doubt these energy exchanges were real for me.

Einstein explained that matter is mostly made up of space. Because ether is space within atoms, vibration can occur. In physics, this vibration is called a "resonant frequency." Everything is energy, frequency, and vibration. When something of a pure higher vibration is introduced to something with a lower vibration, the lower vibrational object always experiences a raise in their vibration if summation occurs. Because crystals and oils and sounds have such unwavering frequencies, when we subject our bodies with these frequencies, it makes our lower vibration rise to the higher frequencies of these substances.

It turned out, I was a natural. Whether it was sound healing, light healing, energy work, crystal therapy, aroma therapy, thought work, or meditation, I was a sponge for everything I learned. Where my career in science and my relationships in the past often felt like a hard slog, with this work, everything I was learning felt easy and fun.

I used to call it the curse of the renaissance man, that desire to learn everything, do everything, and to continually try new things! I mean, I get it. Focusing on many things can be distracting as in the old adage "Jack of all trades, and master of none."

We often make an enemy of ourselves. We abandon ourselves. We hate our opinions and we push our desires aside (and for energy-sensitives, like me, we just suck at honoring our internal boundaries). So, last year, after my largest battle with panic attacks at my Research and Development job at the Buffalo Cancer institute, I decided to say "fuck it" to the wishes people had for me and I started to *solely* move in the direction of what I wanted. I followed my positive emotions.

Pretty soon, my world started to change *quickly*. I got laid off, both romantic and personal relationships ended, and I started to look inside of myself for all of my guidance.

Things got really simple at that point. What I *really* wanted to do was to create freely! So I did just that. I started to blog and create videos – nothings was out of bounds. I created calligraphy videos, became a Reiki Master, and pursued Holistic Health – I embarked on a journey to heal myself *while* having fun in the process.

Then, out of nowhere, an ad for The Author's Way popped up on a YouTube video I was watching. Within nine weeks, I was the author of a manuscript on panic attacks and anxiety!

All I did was *show up* and move toward what felt fun and easy!

I was excelling at many things and listening for my true calling when the book project kicked off. I knew eventually I would need to get back to work and the program taught me exactly how to use a book to build a coaching business. Within a few weeks I had my first clients and I loved working with them. I showed up for myself, my new clients, and the program, and then out of nowhere, I thought "wouldn't it be great to work for a company like this, where I could create content and also coach and also be myself?"

Earlier in the book, I talked about the power of synchronicities. Well, it turned out, at that exact moment I had that thought, the CEO of The Author Incubator, my coach, Dr. Angela Lauria posted on Facebook that she was looking to fill at role just like that. It was like I had been reading her thoughts on our last coaching call.

It was a total "Pinch me!" moment. I would never have imagined that something like this was possible – that I could write, create, lead, and literally enjoy work because it felt like *play*! My office is filled with my favorite crystals, essential oils, and love, and I get to write and connect with people in a way that makes a *difference*! Many authors deal with anxiety or panic as writing their book brings their true purpose into conflict with people and things that are not serving them. All the tools I had to learn to cure my own panic attacks and to write this book are the exact requirements of my job here at The Author Incubator.

Is this real? Is this happening? Am I really a bestselling author working a place that helps create bestselling authors?

I would say that the power of focus is magical!

All I did was press stop on my panic button and press start on trusting myself!

ACKNOWLEDGEMENTS

To Bill, Patty, and Tom. I want to thank you for being my first Reiki clients. You saw my calling and the work I was doing, and you trusted me with your situations. Thank you for the business advice and support. I would say more, but I want to keep you guys as anonymous as possible. You know exactly how much I love you guys! I carry you in my heart forever.

To Nicoal, thank you for all the sidebar conversations and for listening to my sob stories. You authentically held space for me at work when you didn't have to. As simple as that was, your times in our secret hiding space made a world of difference to me! Thank you, hun! My heart melts thinking about you! Love!

To my first coaching client (you know who you are) BIG thank you for trusting me with you panics. From our first conversation I knew we would have a life-long relationship. It was so magical watching you transform from panic paralysis to a rockin' roller! I am so proud of your hard work. You are a beautiful soul and it was my privilege to serve you!

I have never met a sale person I liked until I met a woman by the name of BIG LOVE. Heather, thank you for helping me see where I was, where I wanted to be, and providing the avenue for me to get there.

There is no wonder why I teared up with my first in-person hug from you. I LOVE your love!

To Dr. Angela Lauria, BIG thanks to you! But not in the way you would expect to hear from many others. I suppose people would say thanks for the coaching and for holding space for my transformation. To that I say, "Sure." But what I actually want to say thank you for is your alignment with yourself. That is what I honor about you most. It is through your alignment with yourself that you were able to see me through the eyes of love so we can synchronistically come together to co-create. Your authenticity makes my eyes tear and my heart throb with big love. I am forever transformed because you were in alignment. It was your message, in your words, in the way only YOU could deliver them, that changed my life forever. However raw and unedited, your channeled work is exactly what I needed. Thank you.

ABOUT THE
AUTHOR

Once plagued by panic attacks himself, Ramses Rodriguez now helps individuals suffering from panic and anxiety with holistic modalities. Ramses holds a Master of Science Degree from SUNY Fredonia and combines science theory and alternative therapies to help people remain panic-free while keeping the creative career of their dreams. He now lives in Northern Virginia after landing his creative dream job at The Author Incubator in Georgetown, D.C.

ABOUT DIFFERENCE PRESS

Difference Press offers entrepreneurs, including life coaches, healers, consultants, and community leaders, a comprehensive solution to get their books written, published, and promoted. A boutique-style alternative to self-publishing, Difference Press boasts a fair and easy-to-understand profit structure, low-priced author copies, and author-friendly contract terms. Its founder, Dr. Angela Lauria, has been bringing to life the literary ventures of hundreds of authors-in-transformation since 1994.

LET'S MAKE A DIFFERENCE WITH YOUR BOOK

You've seen other people make a difference with a book. Now it's your turn. If you are ready to stop watching and start taking massive action, reach out.

"Yes, I'm ready!"

In a market where hundreds of thousands books are published every year and are never heard from again, all participants of The Author Incubator have bestsellers that are actively changing lives and making a difference.

"In two years we've created over 250 bestselling books in a row, 90% from first-time authors." We do this by selecting the highest quality and highest potential applicants for our future programs.

Our program doesn't just teach you how to write a book—our team of coaches, developmental editors, copy editors, art directors, and marketing experts incubate you from book idea to published bestseller, ensuring that the book you create can actually make a difference in the world. Then we give you the training you need to use your book to make the difference you want to make in the world, or to create a business out of serving your readers. If you have life-or world-changing ideas or services, a servant's heart, and the willingness to do what it REALLY takes to make a difference in the world with your book, go to http://theauthorincubator.com/apply/ to complete an application for the program today.

OTHER BOOKS BY DIFFERENCE PRESS

Homebuyer Rollercoaster: A Buyer's Guide to Saving Your Money and Sanity

by Monica Benitez & Bebe Bengochea

Thrive in Your Healing Business: Do the Work You Love without Sacrificing Yourself

by Heather Glidden

Chronic Pleasure: Use the Law of Attraction to Transform Fatigue and Pain into Vibrant Energy

by Karen Lorre

The Craft Cannabis Revolution: Succeed as a Small Business in a Giant Industry

by Jonathan Collier

Radical Integrity: 7 Breakthrough Strategies for Transforming Your Business, Sales and Life

by James Jacobi

Pain-Free Everyday: The Roadmap for Natural Treatment When Pills, Injections, or Surgery Aren't Your Solutions

by Eileen Paulo

Love Letters to a Stripper: Create a Future That Will Have You Ditching the Desperation of Dancing

by Angelina Lombardo